T0144958

LUNCH TIME

BY **ANTOINETTE MCDONALD**

Illustrated by Hilbert Bermejo

To order additional copies of this book, contact:
Xlibris
1-888-795-4274
www.Xlibris.com
Orders@Xlibris.com

Dedication

This book is dedicated to the Holy Spirit who gives me every word, to my parents, Ethel and William McDonald who always encouraged me to pursue my dreams, my Aunt, Lenell Grier, who opened the door to my teaching career, and to Nettie McCrory, the most supportive director and mentor one could hope for.

LUNCH TIME

BY

ANTOINETTE MCDONALD

Ms. Miller was asking her last question to the children sitting in group.

It was 11:30 am and the end of story time.

It was LUNCH TIME!

Ms. Sea once again had gotten the class off the **hook,**

When they all stopped listening,
turning around to **look**.

We washed our hands and sat down to **eat,**

Then Diana said,
"what is that **meat?**"

Then Janet said, "I don't eat **that!**"
And Cayla chimed in, "potatoes make you **fat.**"

Brian<u>ne</u> with two n's dug in as she always **do**,
Bria<u>na</u> with one "n" nibbled one bite and said,
"I'm **through**."

Isaiah said "I think this is scrumptious, I like potatoes a **lot.**"

Abraham said, "my mom cooks potatoes in a big **pot.**"

Anori dropped his meat on the floor because he kept turning **around,**
Natalie was slurping her milk and Ms. Smith said, "Please don't make that **sound.**"

Zoe was looking under the table
because she dropped her **fork**.
Nehemiah said, "this ain't chicken, it taste like **pork**."

All the children laughed because they thought that was **funny.**
Anyiah said, "Did this food really cost **money?**"

Ikira said
"let's have a
milk contest cause
I want a **sticker**."

Cindy said, "I'm not drinking my milk, my stomach hurts and it will make me **sicker**."

As lunch time ended and all the children finished picking over their **lunch**, Nikiyiah said, "Ms. Miller, at home I can drink **punch**".

And this is how lunch is **done**,
On a typical day at Kidz Are **Fun.**

Printed in the United States
By Bookmasters